Inventors and Inventions

Teaching Tips

Lime Level 11

This book focuses on developing reading independence, fluency, and comprehension.

Before Reading

- Ask readers what they think the book will be about based on the title. Have them support their answer.

Read the Book

- Encourage readers to read silently on their own.
- As readers encounter unfamiliar words, ask them to look for context clues to see if they can figure out what the words mean. Encourage them to locate boldfaced words in the glossary and ask questions to clarify the meaning of new vocabulary.
- Allow readers time to absorb the text and think about each chapter.
- Ask readers to write down any questions they have about the book's content.

After Reading

- Ask readers to summarize the book.
- Encourage them to point out anything they did not understand and ask questions.
- Ask readers to review the questions on page 23. Have them go back through the book to find answers. Have them write their answers on a separate sheet of paper.

© 2024 Booklife Publishing
This edition is published by arrangement with Booklife Publishing.

North American adaptations © 2024 Jump!
5357 Penn Avenue South
Minneapolis, MN 55419
www.jumplibrary.com

Decodables by Jump! are published by Jump! Library.
All rights reserved. No part of this book may be reproduced in any form without written permission from the publisher.

Library of Congress Cataloging-in-Publication Data is available at www.loc.gov or upon request from the publisher.

ISBN: 979-8-88524-814-3 (hardcover)
ISBN: 979-8-88524-815-0 (paperback)
ISBN: 979-8-88524-816-7 (ebook)

Photo Credits

Images are courtesy of Shutterstock.com. With thanks to Getty Images, Thinkstock Photo and iStockphoto. Cover – lassedesign, Kwirry, MSSA, sraphotohut, StudioG. p4–5 –Fasttailwind, Kokhanchikov. p6–7 -Alison restrepo quiroga, James S. Davis. p8–9 – Kaca Skokanova. p10–11 – Feng Yu, HDesert. p12–13 – Glen Bowman, Tiger Images. p14–15 –metamorworks, drserg. p16–17 – ifong, A Daily Odyssey, Daniel Brasil. p18–19 – Avery Slack, Steve Mann. p20–21 – Juan Ci, Pangog200.

Table of Contents

Page 4   Inventors and Inventions

Page 6   Famous Inventors

Page 8   Moving Around

Page 10   At Home

Page 12   Chocolate

Page 14   The Internet

Page 16   Lucky Accidents

Page 18   Weird and Wacky

Page 20   Young Inventors

Page 22   Index

Page 23   Questions

Page 24   Glossary

Inventors and Inventions

Inventions are completely new things. The people who have the ideas and create these inventions are called **inventors**. Some inventions make our lives easier. Others keep us safe or help us keep in touch with one another.

Almost everything you see, from paper to computers, has been invented by someone who had a clever idea.

People have been inventing things for thousands of years. For example, ancient Romans invented a type of heating for homes, and wigs were invented by ancient Egyptians!

Some inventors spend a very long time working on their ideas. James Dyson took 15 years and thousands of attempts to make a vacuum cleaner that was good enough to sell.

Famous Inventors

Some inventors stand out from the rest because of their brilliant inventions and because they invented so many things.

Leonardo da Vinci invented lots of incredible machines. It is thought that he built a type of robot knight in 1495. He also thought of a machine like a helicopter hundreds of years before the helicopter was invented.

Grace Hopper was an American **mathematician** and part of the U.S. Navy. Hopper invented some clever technology that let computers understand different instructions. This changed how computers worked forever. Hopper also helped make the first computer that you could buy in stores. It was called UNIVAC I.

Moving Around

Have you ever thought about how bicycles were invented? At the end of the 1800s, inventor James Starley created a type of penny-farthing bicycle. Penny-farthings had large front wheels and small back wheels. After the penny-farthing, Starley's nephew invented the "safety bicycle." It had two wheels that were the same size. Lighter mountain bikes were invented in the 1970s.

Penny-farthing bicycle

Some inventions made cars safer. Windshield wipers were invented in 1903 by Mary Anderson. The idea came to her on a snowy car trip when her driver had to keep stopping to clear snow from the windshield.

Garrett Morgan

Garrett Morgan invented traffic lights that use three lights. This made driving much safer.

At Home

Have you ever tried to walk around your home in the dark? If so, you will understand why the invention of the light bulb was so important! In 1879, Thomas Edison perfected the light bulb. It was bright and lasted a long time.

Before light bulbs were invented, many people used candles or oil lamps to see in the dark.

In 1947, Valerie Hunter Gordon began making diapers that could be thrown away. She used cotton wool with a cover made from old nylon parachutes. Her idea was developed in the 1950s, and her diapers soon went on sale.

In 1775, Alexander Cumming invented the first modern flushing toilet. It kept water in the toilet bowl to block nasty smells.

Chocolate

Did you know that chocolate was only a drink before it became a sweet snack? In 1847, Joseph Fry invented something that is still loved today. He mixed sugar with cocoa butter and cocoa powder and pressed the mixture into **molds** to set. These became the first chocolate bars.

Chocolate chip cookies are a very tasty treat. But did you know they were invented by accident? In 1938, Ruth Wakefield ran out of cocoa powder while making chocolate cookies. Instead, she used broken chunks of chocolate. The short baking time meant that the chunks did not melt. She had accidentally invented chocolate chip cookies!

The Internet

A group of computers all linked together is called a **network**. The internet is a giant network of computers that are linked to each other and share information. It began in 1969 as a network of just four computers in the United States. It was called ARPANET.

The first email was sent using ARPANET in 1971.

Computer scientist Tim Berners-Lee realized that a worldwide network of computers would let people around the world connect with each other. He invented something to help computers share information. His invention became known as the World Wide Web. This is what the "www" stands for in web addresses.

Tim Berners-Lee

Lucky Accidents

Cornflakes were invented when John and Will Kellogg accidentally let boiled wheat go stale. Instead of wasting it, they passed it through machines called rollers, hoping to make dough. Instead, they accidentally made flakes. They then tried again with other grains, including corn. The cornflakes became very popular.

George de Mestral invented Velcro in 1955 after a lucky accident. The prickly heads of certain plants got stuck on his pants and in his dog's fur during a walk. After looking closely at the hooks on the plants, he invented a hook and loop fastener for fabrics, which we now call Velcro.

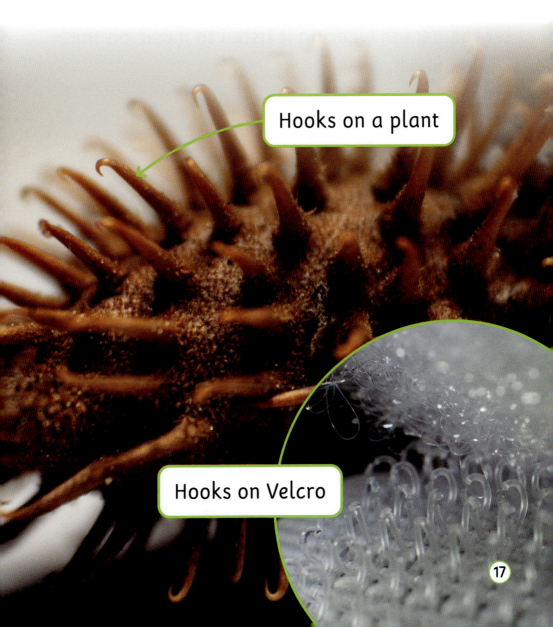

Hooks on a plant

Hooks on Velcro

Weird and Wacky

Some inventions are very clever and can change lots of people's lives. Other inventions are simply weird and wacky! The Man from Mars Radio Hat was designed in 1949 by Victor Hoeflich. In the days before **portable** speakers, this hat let the person wearing it listen to music on the radio anywhere.

The Anti-theft Lunch Bag is a clear plastic bag printed with a picture of **mold** on it. It makes the sandwich inside look moldy so that nobody will want to steal it!

The Sinclair C5 was like a car but for just one person. It was a big failure because it didn't protect anyone from wind or rain, and people did not feel safe driving it.

Young Inventors

Many inventions were created by young people. Louis Braille was blind from a young age. This meant he could not see. When he was 15, he invented a way of reading and writing called braille. Braille uses six bumps in different patterns to mean different letters. A person uses their fingertips to feel the dots and read.

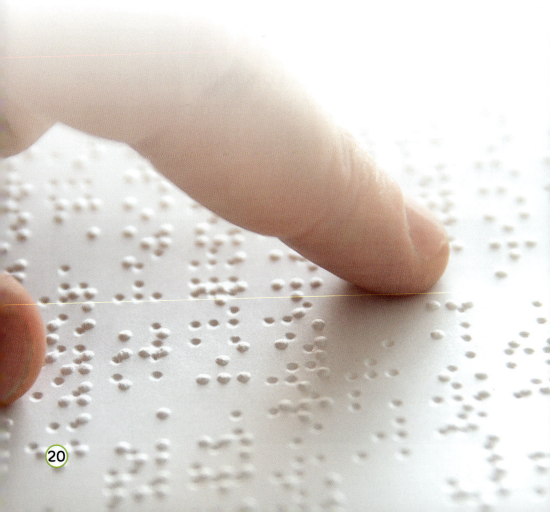

Deepika Kurup was born in 1998. She invented a way to clean water using a material that uses sunlight to make water safer to drink. Her invention doesn't cost too much money to use. This means it could bring clean drinking water to people all around the world.

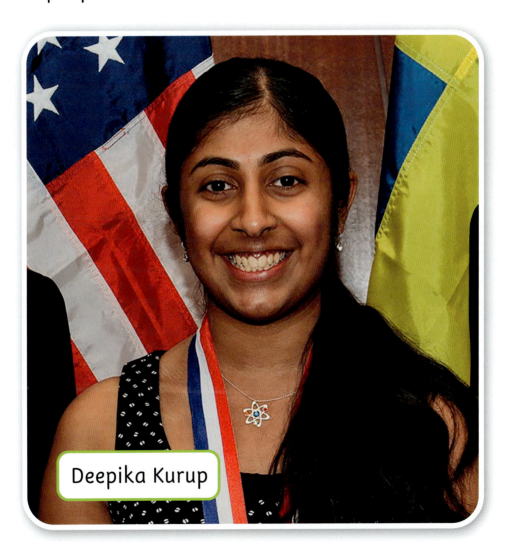

Deepika Kurup

Index

ancient Egyptians 5

ancient Romans 5

bicycles 8

cars 9, 19

clothes 17

computers 4, 7, 14–15

food 12–13, 16, 19

robots 6

teenagers 20–21

toilets 11

How to Use an Index

An index helps us find information in a book. Each word has a set of page numbers. These page numbers are where you can find information about that word.

Page numbers

Example: balloons 5, 8–10, 19

Important word

This means page 8, page 10, and all the pages in between. Here, it means pages 8, 9, and 10.

Questions

1. What is an invention?

2. What did Louis Braille invent?

3. Which type of chocolate was invented first: the drink or the snack?

4. Can you use the Table of Contents to find information about inventions that happened by accident?

5. Can you use the Index to find a page in the book about food?

6. Using the Glossary, can you define what an inventor is?

Glossary

inventions:
Newly designed or created things that are useful.

inventors:
People who think up and create new things.

mathematician:
An expert in mathematics.

mold:
A kind of fungus that grows on old food or things that are warm and moist.

molds:
Containers in particular shapes that you can pour liquid into so that it sets in those shapes.

network:
A group of connected computers or communications equipment.

portable:
Able to be carried or moved easily.